KT-584-686

Ancient Greek Jobs

Haydn Middleton

Heinemann
LIBRARY

500 874 359

www.heinemann.co.uk/library
Visit our website to find out more information about **Heinemann Library** books.

To order:
☎ Phone 44 (0) 1865 888066
🖹 Send a fax to 44 (0) 1865 314091
💻 Visit the Heinemann Bookshop at www.heinemann.co.uk/library to browse our catalogue and order online.

First published in Great Britain by Heinemann Library, Halley Court, Jordan Hill, Oxford OX2 8EJ, a division of Reed Educational and Professional Publishing Ltd. Heinemann is a registered trademark of Reed Educational & Professional Publishing Limited.

OXFORD MELBOURNE AUCKLAND JOHANNESBURG BLANTYRE
GABORONE IBADAN PORTSMOUTH NH (USA) CHICAGO

© Reed Educational and Professional Publishing Ltd 2002.
The moral right of the proprietor has been asserted.

All rights reserved. No part of this publication may be reproduced, stored in a retrieval system, or transmitted in any form or by any means, electronic, mechanical, photocopying, recording, or otherwise without either the prior written permission of the Publishers or a licence permitting restricted copying in the United Kingdom issued by the Copyright Licensing Agency Ltd, 90 Tottenham Court Road, London W1P 0LP.

Designed by Tinstar Design (www.tinstar.co.uk)
Illustrations by Jeff Edwards and Art Construction.
Originated by Ambassador Litho Ltd.
Printed by Wing King Tong in Hong Kong.

ISBN 0 431 14543 1 (hardback)   ISBN 0 431 14548 2   (paperback)
06 05 04 03 02   07 06 05 04 03
10 9 8 7 6 5 4 3 2 1   10 9 8 7 6 5 4 3 2 1

British Library Cataloguing in Publication Data
Middleton, Haydn
     Ancient Greek jobs. – (People in the past)
     1. Occupations – Greece – History – To 1500 – Juvenile literature
     2. Greece – Civilization – To 146 B.C. – Juvenile literature
     I.Title
     331.7'0938

Acknowledgements
The Publishers would like to thank the following for permission to reproduce photographs: AKG London pp7, 8, 13, 14, 17, 20, 23, 24, 32, 33, 34, 39, Ancient art and architecture collection pp6, 12, 16, 22, 25, 28, 30, 37, 38, 40, CM Dixon p11, Michael Holford pp19, 36, Richard Butler and Magnet Harlequin p41, SCALA p26.

Cover photograph reproduced with permission of AKG (Erich Lessing).

The Publishers would like to thank Dr Michael Vickers of the Ashmolean Museum, Oxford, for his assistance in the preparation of this book.

Every effort has been made to contact copyright holders of any material reproduced in this book. Any omissions will be rectified in subsequent printings if notice is given to the Publisher.

Words appearing in the text in bold, **like this**, are explained in the Glossary.

Contents

The ancient-Greek world

When people talk about ancient Greece, they do not just mean the modern-day country of Greece as it used to be. The ancient-Greek world was made up of the hot, rocky mainland of Greece, plus hundreds of islands in the Aegean, Ionian and Adriatic Seas, with further overseas settlements in places ranging from northern Africa to what we now call Turkey and Italy. The earliest Greek-speakers did not think they all belonged to a single country. For a long while they did not even think they all belonged to the same **civilization**.

From Minoans to Macedonians

For centuries the mightiest people in the Greek world were the Minoans, based on the island of Crete. Power then passed to the warlike Mycenaeans, based on the mainland region known as the **Peloponnese**. This was followed around the year 1100 BC by centuries of confusion and upheaval, but since the art of writing was also lost, we know very little about it. In the later 'Classical Age', from about 500 BC until about 300 BC, prosperity was restored by the rise of many city-states like Athens. Most of the information in this book is about life in the city-states in this period. The Greek word for city-state was *polis*. Each *polis* controlled the villages and farmland around it. Each had its own laws and customs, and often they fought bitter wars against each other.

Daily life differed from one city-state to the next, but most of the men in them worked on the land as farmers. In the cities, other jobs needed to be done too – ranging from banking and sculpting to teaching and trading at the market. As you will discover, however, Greek people used to have different ideas about what kinds of work it was 'honourable' to do. Some philosophers even thought that citizens – who ran the *polis* – should not be distracted by work at all!

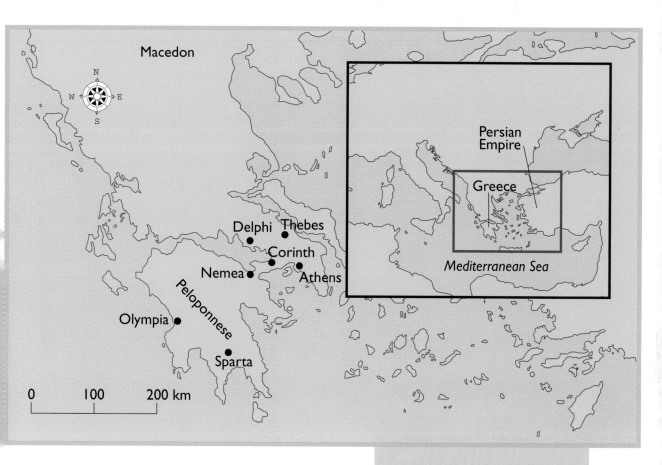

All Greeks were united by their common language and by their belief that their ways were superior to those of any foreign **barbarians**. Today – more than 2000 years since the Greek world was finally united under Alexander the Great before becoming a part of the Roman Empire – ancient-Greek words, ideas, art-forms and attitudes still have a deep effect on us all.

Ancient Greece was not a single unified country but a collection of many separate states that often waged war on one another. The ancient Greeks used the word *Hellas* to mean all the places where there was a Greek way of life.

Who worked in ancient Greece?

The picture above shows the Erechtheion, a marvellous temple in Athens. Records survive from 405 BC, telling us who built it. There were 71 men under contract – 20 **citizens** of Athens, 35 *metics* (or foreigners living in Athens) and 16 slaves. Of the foremen on the job, three were citizens, two were *metics* and one was a slave. All of them – free and unfree alike – were paid at the same rate. This was a **drachma** a day for a skilled worker – twice what an unskilled man might earn.

Did many citizens work?

We do not always know exactly who worked on such big public projects, or what they were all paid. It is harder still to discover details about the many lesser craftsmen and tradesmen who worked in their own homes or in rough buildings attached to them. We can guess that most worked only during daylight hours (there was no electric lighting!) and not on festival days, which differed from place to place. We *do* know that some great ancient-Greek writers believed that freeborn citizens should not work at all.

This vase painting shows a shoemaker at work. He is pictured working alone, which might mean that he specialized in one area of shoemaking (see page 28).

According to the writer Aristotle, citizens should not work 'since leisure is necessary both for the development of virtue and the performance of political duties.' You can find out what some of these duties were on the next page.

In Classical Athens, many citizens did not actually need to work. Their incomes came from owning land, from letting out city properties, or owning small 'factories' and workshops. Some citizens did work, like weavers and sculptors, but they still enjoyed high **status**. However, no Athenian citizen would willingly work for long as a wage-earning employee for another citizen. By working for a master, he might seem to others to be little better than a slave (see page 10). Although women did all kinds of domestic work, few did the sort of wage-earning work that men did. Their place was believed to be in the home. There was no such thing as equal opportunities in ancient Greece!

Early risers

In *The Birds*, a play by Aristophanes, one of the characters listed all the types of workers who had to make an early start: 'When the cock sings his dawn song, up they all jump and rush off to work, the bronze-smiths, the potters, the tanners, the shoemakers, the bath-attendants, the corn-merchants, the **lyre**-shapers and shield-makers, and some of them even put on their sandals and leave when it's still dark.' The Athenian historian Xenophon had no time for many of the craftsmen listed here, he wrote: 'The bodies of those who do this work are damaged, since they are forced to sit down and work indoors. Some people even have to spend all day at the fire. As their bodies grow soft, so do their **characters**.'

The citizen

'Man is above all a political animal,' wrote Aristotle. The ancient Greeks took their politics very seriously, experimenting with all forms of government from monarchy and **aristocracy** to **anarchy**. Many of the political terms we use today – including 'politics' itself – come from ancient-Greek words. The **citizens** of each *polis* usually had at least some say in how they were governed. From c.500 BC in Athens they had more say than most. That was when and where 'democracy' was invented. According to US President Abraham Lincoln, democracy is 'government of the people, by the people, for the people.' Whereas in modern **democracies**, millions of people vote in elections for others to govern them, in Classical Athens the few thousand citizens did the governing themselves. For that reason, to be a citizen was a vitally important job.

Direct democracy

The citizens' assembly, the *ecclesia*, met about forty times a year – on a hill outside Athens called the Pnyx. After some opening prayers, every citizen, rich or poor, was allowed to speak up. Debates on big issues like whether Athens should go to war could be turbulent. Meetings of the *ecclesia* were organized by the *boule*, a council of 500 elected members who all had to serve for a year.

Pericles (c.495–429 BC) was a very important politician in Athens from 443 BC until his death. His brilliant speeches greatly influenced the citizens' decisions.

The *boule* met on every day that was not a festival day. Among other duties it supervised various boards of five or ten officials who kept the city running smoothly. There were boards to inspect weights and measures, to ensure that the roads were repaired, and to make sure that religious festivals were properly celebrated. In *The Constitution of Athens*, it was recorded that the board of the ten *astynomoi* had to check 'that none of the dung-collectors dump dung within two kilometres of the city-wall. They also prevent the extending of houses into, and the building of balconies over, the streets … And they see to it that the girls who play the flute, the harp and the **lyre** are not hired for more than two **drachmas**.'

As well as serving as council members and public officials, each year citizens also had to take their turn to be jurymen – to give verdicts on quarrels between other citizens. They were given small sums to cover their expenses, but the rate of pay was poor – only half the amount paid to the skilled workers who built the Erechtheion at the **Acropolis** in Athens.

Roping in and voting out

Meetings of the *ecclesia* needed a **quorum** of 6000 citizens. Sometimes, since these meetings were held early in the day, or because some citizens were too lazy to go to the Pnyx of their own accord, they had to be 'roped in' from the **agora** – almost literally. Scythian slaves went around touching idle citizens with a rope covered in red chalk or paint. Anyone so marked had to pay a fine. A more serious punishment was 'ostracism'. Once a year, the citizens had a chance to banish anyone they disapproved of. Votes were cast by scratching a name on a broken piece of pottery. If a total of 6000 pieces was collected up, the person with most votes against him had to leave the city for ten years.

The slave

In 5th-century BC Athens there were maybe 80,000 – 100,000 slaves. Some experts believe there were many more. That was at least one slave for every free member of the population. Most of them were foreign – **Persians** or Asians captured during warfare; some were the children of slave-parents. Slaves in Sparta, Thessaly or Sicily often led hard lives, but in Athens it could be difficult to tell who was a slave and who was free.

A world without slaves

In his comedy *The Wild Animals*, the playwright Crates mocked the idea of a **Utopia**, where there were no male or female slaves. In that case, he said, all the household chores would have to do themselves. You can see what some were from his list: laying the table, kneading dough, pouring wine, washing cups, making bread, serving beef, cooking fish.

'There is a very great lack of discipline among the slaves and *metics* in Athens,' wrote historian Xenophon. 'You are not allowed to strike a slave there, nor will a slave step aside for you … Ordinary **citizens** there wear no better clothes than slaves or *metics*, and look no different.' This may well have been true of domestic slaves and some citizens bought slaves 'to share their work with them', so they probably treated them decently too. There were even some slaves who lived apart from their masters, paid them a proportion of their earnings, and saved up the rest to buy their freedom one day.

Human tools

The philosopher Aristotle called a slave 'a living tool'. Masters could treat their slaves as they chose – and only a foolish master would choose to maltreat his own tools. However, in the silver-mines at Laurion in south-eastern Attica, it was a different story.

There, slaves probably outnumbered the free inhabitants. Thousands of them worked in appalling conditions underground. Kneeling or lying flat in tunnels just a metre square, they had to dig out the ore by the light of small clay oil-lamps. Other workers then dragged the silver ore away to the main shaft and carried it up a wooden staircase to the workshops to be washed. Afterwards it was **smelted** on the same site, giving rise to foul toxic fumes. Many slaves from here must have been among the 20,000 who – according to Athenian historian Thucydides – escaped to Sparta towards the end of the **Peloponnesian** War (431–404 BC). In 135 BC, there was a rare outbreak of mass violence involving over a thousand slaves. They were ruthlessly crushed before the trouble could spread.

This vase image from c.340 BC shows a domestic slave attending the mistress of her household. She might also be sent to market to shop for food.

The priest and priestess

Ancient Greece was a land full of **deities**. Some were worshipped in the home, some in particular cities, some throughout the Greek-speaking world. Temples dotted the landscape, and the calendar was full of sacred festivals. Yet the priests who organized all this religious activity were not specially trained experts. They were just ordinary **citizens**, chosen to do the job part-time. They were more like **civil servants** than professional holy men.

Getting the rituals right

In Athens, more than forty priestesses were employed at major **shrines**, and some great festivals like the *Thesmophoria* were celebrated only by women. To be a priestess was the only public job a woman could do. Male priests usually carried out sacrifices, while priestesses might weave clothes for temple statues. The main role of both was to carry out all the necessary rituals, in the right order, at the right time. If they did not, the deities might turn against the city.

Particular gods or goddesses were worshipped in Greek temples. This one, built by Greeks in Italy, was dedicated to the sea-god Poseidon, known later to the Romans as Neptune.

These rituals could be odd. This was how the *Dipolia* festival was celebrated: 'They selected girls named water-carriers. They carried water so that the men could sharpen the axe and the knife. Of the men who did the sharpening one passed the axe, a second struck the ox, a third slit its throat. After this they skinned it and everyone had a share of the meat. When this was over they sewed up the ox hide, stuffed it with straw and stood it up, looking just as it did in life ... They then held a trial for murder [of the ox] and summoned all those who took part in the operation to make their defence. The water-carriers put the blame on those who did the sharpening. The sharpeners accused the man who handed over the axe, he blamed the man who struck the blow, he blamed the man who slit the throat, and he said the knife itself was guilty. Since the knife was incapable of speech, it was condemned for murder.' (Porphyry)

A sacrifice, to the god Apollo, is being made here. A priest would offer an animal's bones and inedible parts to the gods, while the edible meat was cooked and eaten.

Calling down curses

Priests and priestesses aimed to please their people's gods. They also tried to get these gods to punish the people's enemies. Around 470 BC, the priests of the city of Teos in Ionia devised a curse on anyone who used poison against the Teians, prevented corn supplies from coming in, or betrayed the city in various other ways. The curse was then inscribed on stone, and had to be uttered at three big festivals – the spring festival of *Anthesteria*, and the festivals of Heracles and of Zeus. We cannot be sure how effective the curse was!

The teacher

There was not a great demand for teachers in ancient Greece. Only well-off **citizens** sent their sons to school, and usually they kept their daughters at home to learn the skills they would one day need as wives.

In different city-states there were different education systems. In Sparta, boys from the age of seven were brought up in **barracks**, not in family homes. The aim of Spartan teaching was to produce excellent warriors, and it was overseen by the *paidonomos* – a state director of education. The government of Athens did not run special schools for citizens' sons. It probably did not even insist that they went to school at all. It just laid down laws that boys' journeys to and from the building took place in daylight, and that the pupils aged from seven to fourteen were protected from 'bad influences'.

This young man is writing on a wax plate with an instrument called a stylus.

Who were the teachers?

A *paidagogos*, or tutor, might accompany the boy at all times during the school day. He was a slave owned by the boy's father, and was responsible for his behaviour rather than his education. A *grammatistes* would teach the boy reading, writing and simple arithmetic, and get him to learn by heart long passages from great poems like Homer's *Iliad* and *Odyssey*. A *kitharistes* or music-teacher would teach him the **lyre**, the *aulos* (which was like a double oboe) and singing. Then a *paidotribes* would supervise his physical education at the **palaestra**. This kind of 'all-round' education was popular in Athens before c.450 BC. Then teachers began to put more emphasis on writing-style and grammar.

Teachers needed no special qualifications to do their job; anyone could set himself up as a schoolmaster. Teachers' fees from parents seem to have been low, and so was their **status**. In the 4th century BC the great public speaker Demosthenes once taunted an opponent by saying: 'Your childhood was spent in an atmosphere of great poverty. You had to help your father in his job as assistant teacher – preparing the ink, washing down the benches, sweeping out the class-room, and taking the rank of a slave rather than a freeborn boy.'

Jokes about teachers

The abilities of ancient-Greek teachers must have varied from school to school. Some did not have a high reputation among other citizens. Stories went around ridiculing the *scholastikos* – a kind of nutty professor. In his book *Europe*, the modern historian Norman Davies records some of the stories. One told how a *scholastikos* wanted to see what he looked like when he was asleep – so he stood in front of a mirror with his eyes shut!

The doctor

'We physicians base our diagnosis on our general knowledge of disease, and of particular diseases, and on our special knowledge of the illness we are treating, of the patient, his previous history and his previous doctor. Factors include the climate, the patient's origin, his way of life, his work, his age, his conversation, his **idiosyncracies**, his silences, his thoughts, his capacity for sleep, his dreams (their number and nature), any picking or scratching, **hysteria**, discharges, sneezing or sickness. We are **meticulous** in noting the progress of the illness to the critical point, checking such details as perspiration, chill, stiffness, coughs or sneezing, hiccoughing, heavy breathing, internal bleeding. It is our professional duty to observe all these factors and their consequences.'

So wrote Hippocrates, who ran a school of medicine on the island of Kos during Classical times. His approach sounds quite similar to that of modern doctors. In fact, many of his ideas had a lasting influence on medical theory and practice. Doctors today still take the 'Hippocratic Oath' (see box).

Painful-looking instruments like these would have been used by ancient-Greek doctors!

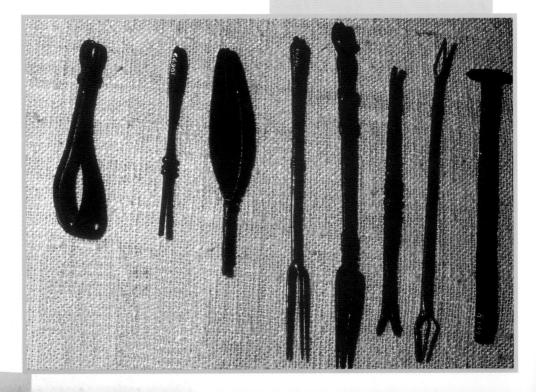

The duties of a doctor

The Hippocratic Oath demanded high standards of personal behaviour from those who intended to earn their living as doctors: 'I will give treatment to help the sick to the best of my ability and judgement … Whatever I see or hear, which should not be spoken to any person outside, I will never **divulge** …' A new doctor also had to swear to 'pass on **precepts**, lectures, and all other learning to my sons, to those of my master, and to those pupils duly apprenticed and sworn, and to none other …'

Before, during and after Hippocrates' time, there were also a lot of non-scientific 'healers' in ancient Greece. 'Witch-doctors, faith-healers, quacks and charlatans,' one writer called them. They relied more on magic than on observation or experience. Yet even 'proper' doctors – who might train for many years under their fathers or masters – took no degrees or other qualifications, so they were judged on the results of their treatments. Since their patients had to pay them for their visits, their **livelihoods** depended on that too!

Celebrity doctors

The effect that most doctors had was limited, for the Greeks had little grasp of the causes of disease, and a **taboo** stopped them from dissecting the human body to find out more about its workings. Some doctors, like Demokedes from Kroton, made great names for themselves – and great wealth. The historian Herodotus recorded that the island of Aegina paid him one *talent* a year as resident physician. That was twenty times as much as an average skilled worker. Then at Samos he was employed at a rate of two *talents* a year.

The medical expert Hippocrates (c.460–c.377 BC) is sometimes called 'the father of medicine' because of the sensible and kind way he treated his patients.

The merchant

From very early times, the Greeks were a busy trading people. Island traded with island, city with city, and Athens was the biggest city of them all. Most trade was carried out by sea, since overland travel was costly and difficult in a land with few good roads. The map below shows how far afield merchants travelled, often to Greek **colonies** in North Africa and Western Europe, and the goods they brought back. In small, slow, rounded wooden vessels with a single mast and a large, square-rigged sail, they braved the seas without charts, compasses or other vital navigational aids.

Risk-taking traders

A merchant was often the owner of a single ship, of which he was the master. If he had no ship, he might hire cargo space from a ship-owner. He might also have to take out a loan, to pay for all or some of the cargo. In that case, he could turn to a banker or money-lender to help him out.

Many merchants were seen as rough-and-ready types, whose only interest lay in making a profit. Often they were foreigners or, in Athens, **metics** – so they did not enjoy high **status**. It is unlikely that they cared much about that. They had enough on their minds already – for with every voyage their goods could be lost in shipwrecks or stolen by pirates, or simply turn out to be unsalable.

N
W E
S

SCYTHIA
timber,
slaves

Olbia

Dioscurias

Massalia

ITALY
meat, copper,
wool, linen

THRACE
iron, copper,
grain, slaves

Odessus

Sinope
iron, fish,
nuts

Neapolis   MACEDONIA
timber, gold,
Sybaris   silver

Heraclea

Croton

Phoecaea

ASIA MINOR

Selinus

Sicily   Syracuse
grain,
timber,

Corinth   Athens
oil, wine,
Sparta   silver, pottery,
metalwork

Miletus

Phaselis

Al Mina

CARTHAGE
rugs, cushions

Rhodes

Crete

Cyprus   Salamis
grain, oil,
timber,
copper

SYRIA
slaves,
dates,
dyes

Cyrene
wool, grain,
silphium,
vegetables

Naucratis

● Greek homeland cities
● Greek colonies

EGYPT
grain, papyrus,
flax, ivory

These were the main Greek colonies in the Mediterranean and Black Seas. You can see what goods they produced, then traded between them.

Historians once thought that traders always 'hugged' the coasts on their voyages and sailed, if possible, only during the day. In 2001, archaeologists discovered a sunken Greek trading ship between Rhodes and Alexandria, right in the middle of the Mediterranean Sea. Four similar wrecks are believed to lie nearby. More discoveries like this may one day prove that really **intrepid** Greek traders often made long-distance voyages across open seas too.

Supply and demand

Merchants had to be good businessmen. This often involved buying goods cheaply and selling them on at high prices. The Athenian historian Xenophon wrote of traders who 'from their passion for grain, sail in search of it wherever they hear it is most abundant, crossing over the Aegean, Euxine and Sicilian Seas. And when they have got as much of it as they can, they bring it away over the water, stowing it in the vessel in which they themselves sail. And when they are in want of money, they carry their freight to ... wherever they hear that grain will fetch the highest price, and offer it for sale.'

This vase is decorated with a painting of a merchant ship powered by sail. It was made in c.540 BC.

The banker

'The resources required by those who engage in trade come not from those who borrow, but from those who lend; and neither ship nor ship-owner nor passenger can put to sea, if you take away the part contributed by those who lend.' Not surprisingly, the speaker here was a money-lender, or banker, himself – a man called Chrysippus. He was complaining to a jury in Classical Athens that he had been cheated by a **metic** merchant to whom he had lent 2000 **drachmas**, to finance a trading voyage to the Bosphorus Sea.

Bankers were indeed very important when traders needed large sums of money. They made the most of this by charging high rates of interest for each voyage.

These coins, found with this **terracotta** jug, date back to the 4th century BC. After coins were introduced into Greece from Lydia in about 600 BC, coin hoards like this one were often buried to keep them safe.

Hugely successful slaves

We know of twenty or so bankers in Classical Athens. The most successful was a man called Pasion. Remarkably, he began his working life as another banker's slave. Around 400 BC he gained his freedom, took over his master's business, and even became a **citizen** by a decree of the people, despite his low birth. When he died, it was said he was worth almost 60 *talents*. (In 431 BC there were only 6000 *talents* in the entire Athenian treasury.) Then his own slave Phormio rose to be made a citizen too.

Almost all bankers were *metics*, and many were ex-slaves. Very few followed in the rags-to-riches footsteps of Pasion and Phormio. Their services were used mainly by other *metics*. This was because many citizens preferred to rely on friends, neighbours or relations if they needed to make a deposit or take out a loan. However, citizens might use bankers as money-changers, since so many different coinages were used in the ancient-Greek world.

Banking practices

'When a private individual deposits money with the instruction that it is to be paid to a particular person, the banker begins by writing the depositor's name and the sum of money, and then he writes alongside 'to be paid to X'. If the banker knows by sight the person to whom the payment is to be made, then he just has to write his name. If he does not, he adds the name of a person who will identify and introduce to him the person who is to receive the money.' The Athenian politician Demosthenes recorded this long-winded system, from the days before cheques and cards. To a modern mind, it does not seem very secure.

The farmer

Most Greeks worked on the land, but Greece is not a very fertile country. Only about a fifth of it is cultivated today; in ancient times it was probably the same. Lowland farmers mainly grew grain – barley and wheat – and vines for wine and, most importantly of all, olives. Olive oil was used for cooking, for lamp-fuel, and also as a substitute for soap. Farmers grew so many olives that they had enough for their own needs and then sold the surplus for some extra cash. Farmers on higher ground kept bees for their honey, small numbers of sheep and pigs, and also goats for their milk and cheese. To grow any crops they first had to cut terraces into the rocky mountain slopes – always a tough job.

Farming communities

A few farmers were extraordinarily rich men, who spent most of their time in the city and let **overseers** run their farms. In Classical times a landowner called Phaenippus had an annual income of around 30,000 **drachmas**. (Skilled workmen earned only one *drachma* a day, remember.) Most farmers, however, owned or rented very small farms – maybe only four or five acres in size – and lived together in villages to protect and support one another.

This view of the modern-Greek countryside around Athens, shows one of many regions that must have been hard to farm in ancient times.

Often they struggled to make a living. Poor rainfall in Attica – the region around Athens – meant they might lose their whole wheat crop once every four years. Their aim was to produce enough food for themselves and their families, and then a little more to sell in the nearest city.

City-dwellers depended heavily on what farmers grew, but did not always treat them with a great deal of respect. The teacher and writer Theophrastus made fun of a **rustic** in the late 4th century BC. This country person seems rather innocent, almost childlike: 'If he has lent someone a plough, basket, sickle or bag, he goes to ask for it back in the middle of the night … And when he is going to the city, he asks anyone he meets about the price of hides and salt fish … And he says right away that, when he gets there, he's going to have his hair cut, have his shoes re-soled … and have a good sing in the public baths.'

Farming against the odds

The Greek climate is hot and dry, the landscape is mountainous, and much of the soil is thin and hard to farm. As early as the 6th century BC, Greek rulers tried to make sure that the land was looked after. Farmers were given a reward for planting new olive trees, to keep up their numbers. However, the philosopher Plato wrote: 'What now remains … is like the skeleton of a sick man, all the fat and soft earth having wasted away. There are some mountains which now have nothing but food for bees, but they had trees a year ago, and boundless pastures.'

This vase shows farm-workers picking olives. Olive trees grew well in the poor Greek soil. The trees also provided welcome shade from the hot sun.

23

The fisherman and the fishmonger

One of the great mariners of Greek myth was Odysseus. For ten years after the siege of Troy, he and his men sailed the seas before returning home to Ithaca. His thrilling story is recounted in Homer's epic poem, the *Odyssey*. Scholars have noted that on all their travels, these famous sailors hardly ever seemed to eat fish. When they put ashore, their banquets featured roasted meats instead.

Once, when the sailors landed on the island of the Sun-god's cattle, 'all the food in the ship was gone and they were forced instead to go roaming in search of prey, using bent hooks to catch fish and birds, anything that might come to hand, because hunger gnawed their bellies.' It seems that they looked on fish as poor men's food, not suitable for true **archaic** heroes. This is odd, because by Classical times fish became the most desirable of all foods – which was fortunate, since fish simply teemed in the seas off the many coastlines of Greece.

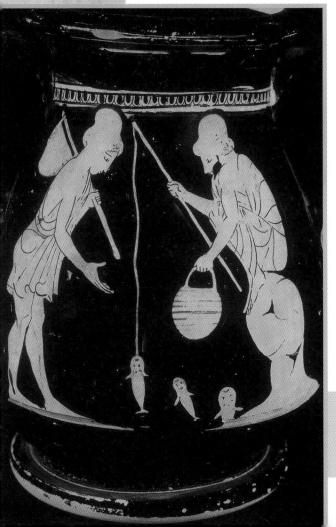

Fishy story

Writers continued to say little about the men who caught these fish. They sold catches of little fish like anchovies and sprats to the poor, and supplied such delicacies as electric rays, tuna, sea bass, red mullet and crayfish to the better off. There were no fridges, so fish had to be sold quickly or 'preserved' in salt, although salt-fish was looked down on as a cheap substitute for the real thing.

Fish-catching techniques seem to have changed remarkably little since ancient-Greek times!

Many fish were baked and served whole. This decorated Greek plate has a small recess or dent at its centre. It was used for storing the sauce that went with the fish.

Although Greek writers largely ignored fishermen, they had plenty to say about fishmongers – usually dishonest ones. In his collection of stories called *The Golden Ass*, Apuleius told how a man haggled with a fishmonger for a basket of fish. He got the price down from 200 to 20 **drachmas**, and paid up, but as he took the basket away, the market inspector intervened. He was so scandalized at the poor quality of the fish, that he emptied the basket on the ground. Then he ordered his officer to jump on them until they were mashed into paste. 'All is well now, Lucius,' he said to the customer. 'That wretched little fishmonger has been humiliated enough.' The customer departed, 'flabbergasted at having lost both his money and his dinner'!

Top fish

Most ancient writers seem to agree that the most highly prized item on any fishmonger's stall was the eel. It was believed that fishermen who trawled the waters between Sicily and the 'toe' of Italy caught the choicest eels. 'All in all I think the eel rules over everything else at the feast,' was the view of the writer Archestratus, 'despite being the only fish with no backbone.'

The market trader

Pausanias defined a city-state as a place that had government offices, a gymnasium, a theatre, an **agora** and a fountain. An *agora* was vital to the life of any Greek city. It is usually translated as 'market-place'. According to the historian Herodotus, the King of Persia called it 'a special place marked out where Greeks meet to cheat each other'!

This vase painting shows a fishmonger chopping up fish for a customer. Fresh fish would have been available to buy daily at the *agora*.

The hub of the city

Craftsmen could sell their wares at the *agora* as well as from their workshops. It was also a place for having meetings, hiring workers, watching entertainment and putting criminals on trial. 'In one and the same place,' wrote the comic poet Eubulus, 'you will find all kinds of things for sale together at Athens: figs, **bailiffs**, bunches of grapes, turnips, pears, apples, witnesses, roses, **medlars**, milk-puddings, honeycombs, chickpeas, lawsuits, **beestings**, curds, myrtle, allotment machines, irises, lambs, water-clocks, laws and **indictments**.'

Different types of goods and services were sold in different parts of the market: olive oil on the east side, barbers on the north side, along with bankers who sat at counters to make loans or change money. The goods were laid out on flimsy stalls, although some traders had small covered shops – the walls and roofs of which, were made of reeds. It must have been hot, dusty and very noisy.

Wealthy women did not visit the *agora* unless they were looking for perfume or fashionable jewellery. Their husbands or slaves did the daily shopping, then had it sent on to the house. There were no shopping bags. Aristophanes described soldiers buying vegetable purée and taking it away in their helmets. Odder still, male Athenian shoppers seem to have carried small change in their mouths. From 374 BC, public 'testers' of silver coins sat every day at a certain spot in the *agora* with weighing scales. The tester was a slave. If he failed to appear, he was beaten with 'fifty strokes' as a reminder to do his duty.

Fair trade?

Customers haggled, or bargained, with stallholders over the prices of their goods. Inevitably – just like in some markets today – there were some dishonest traders around. Greek writers complained about overcharging, and also about the traders' bad backgrounds. Market inspectors tried to ensure fair-trading (see page 25).

The craftsman

The Athenian historian Xenophon wrote: 'In small towns the same person makes doors, beds, ploughs, tables; he's often a builder too; and even so he is delighted if he finds enough work to keep him going. And of course a jack of all trades is master of none. In large cities there are plenty of customers for any one branch of industry, and one branch of industry or even a **subdivision** of it is enough to support an individual. So one worker specializes in male footwear, another in female. In some places one man earns his living by stitching shoes, another by cutting them out, another by simply sewing the **uppers** together, without any specialized skill except rounding the job off. So anyone who is proposing to concentrate on a highly-specialized job is bound to be supremely good at it.'

This painting shows two blacksmiths working at a furnace. Blacksmiths had to heat charcoal, their usual fuel, to high enough temperatures to reduce the ore properly. Otherwise the resulting metal would be impure, which meant it would break easily.

Servicing the rich

Many Greek writers looked down on people who worked with their hands. In an ideal world, a Greek would give his time only to politics or warfare – two supposedly noble pursuits. Only rich landowners could afford to do this. However, some writers pointed out that without manual workers to meet the needs of rich men, their lives would have been very different. In a play by Aristophanes, Chremylus and his slave Cario put their case to a character called Wealth:

'*Chremylus*: Every skill and every invention of mankind is at your service. For you one of us sits making shoes.

Cario: Another works in bronze, another in wood.

Chremylus: Another moulds the gold received from you.

Cario: Another is a **cutpurse**, another a burglar.'

By this last remark, he meant that many kinds of workers – and thieves too – 'served' the rich people who nevertheless looked down on them.

Small-scale industry

In big cities, craftsmen of the same kind had their workshops in a single area. In Athens, the potters' quarter was called the *Kerameikos*. By working so close together they could exchange ideas, and compete to produce the finest wares.

Craftsmen's workshops, even in the cities, were quite small. A *metic* called Kephalos owned an armour-making 'factory' in Athens, and he employed 120 slaves. That was unusual. The father of the Athenian politician Demosthenes ran a workshop with twenty carpenters who made beds; a man named Timarchos ran a business staffed by nine shoemakers and one foreman. Sometimes craftsmen just worked in their own homes, or in buildings added on to them. They could be free men, slaves or *metics*; sometimes all three kinds of men worked under the same roof. The average pay seems to have been a **drachma** a day for a skilled worker, which was what soldiers or sailors on campaign were also paid.

The potter

In Classical times (roughly 500–300 BC), the Greeks did not set artists apart from other workers. Along with blacksmiths, carpenters and shoemakers, they were all involved in *techne* – craft – from which we get our word 'technology'. Some of their handiwork could be so fine that it has survived as the highest art.

Most crafts were practised in families. Boys would naturally become apprentices to their fathers, whose workmen and slaves they would help, and so learn their skills. Usually there were no more than ten men in a workshop. Each town or village would have its own pottery, using local supplies of clay. It mainly served local needs, and often produced vases in styles peculiar to that local area.

From the 6th century BC however, for about 150 years, Athenian pottery (see box) became popular across a very wide area. As pottery does not decay, it has since been found all over the Mediterranean region.

Black figures, red figures

Athenian clay, rich in iron, went a reddish colour when it was fired in a kiln. Before the firing, artists used to decorate their pots with a mixture of clay, water and wood ash, scratching on any details with a pointed tool. After firing, the decorations turned out black and the backgrounds were red. After about 510 BC, a 'red-figure' style became more popular. The backgrounds were black, with figures appearing in red – but with details outlined in black with a fine brush, which gave more fluid lines than a scratching tool.

Practical and beautiful

Pottery objects had all sorts of uses in the home and in religious rituals. Vases were vital containers – for liquids like olive oil or for solids like grain – since the Greeks lacked modern materials like plastics and cardboard. Potters made them in all shapes and sizes, like *amphorae* to store wine in and *kraters* that were cups for wine and water. Those that were painted give us information on all aspects of Greek life.

As in sculpture (see next page), Greek vase painting grew more and more 'realistic' over time. Painters paid special attention to the human figure, and tried to see how people's inner feelings affected the body in action. They aimed, in the words of the philosopher Socrates, 'to represent the workings of the human soul'. In the 5th century BC, some of them produced work to match this ideal.

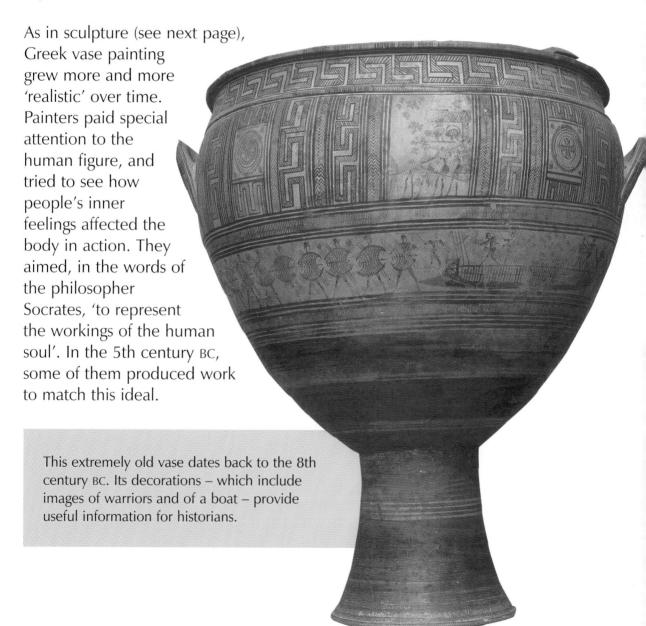

This extremely old vase dates back to the 8th century BC. Its decorations – which include images of warriors and of a boat – provide useful information for historians.

31

The sculptor

'To Phyromachus of Cephisia, for the figure of the young man by the breastplate: 60 **drachmas**.
To Praxias, resident of Melite, for the figures of the horse and the man behind turning it: 120 *drachmas*.
To Antiphanes of Cerameis, for the figures of the chariot, young man and pair of horses being yoked: 240 *drachmas* …'

These are part of the **accounts** for a public building project in Athens in 407 BC. The men being paid were sculptors. They seem to have been paid at a rate of 60 *drachmas* for each figure that they produced, but we cannot say how long each figure took to make. Some of the men in these accounts were not natives of Athens. Good sculptors tended to move around as they plied their trade.

We know the names of some of the most famous Greek sculptors – Polykleitos in the 5th century BC; Praxiteles, Skopas and Lysippos in the 4th – but almost none of their masterpieces have survived. This is because sculptors most usually worked in stone, which breaks quite easily, or in bronze, which was often later melted down and re-used for other purposes. Fortunately Roman copies of some great sculptures do still exist.

The elusive Phidias

The biggest and greatest surviving sculptures are the marble decorations of the Parthenon (see page 42). Its **frieze** was a continuous band 525 feet (160 metres) long, and there were also two beautifully decorated **pediments**. All this work was carried out in less than ten years from c.440 to 432 BC, so several master sculptors must have been involved. Their **overseer** was called Phidias.

A statue of a boxer from the 1st century BC is shown here. The signature of the sculptor – Appollonis, son of Nestor – appears on the thongs wrapped around the boxer's hands.

This magnificent statue dates back to the 1st century BC. Made from a single block of marble, it shows the mythical Laocoon and his sons being squeezed to death by serpents. In was discovered in a Roman vineyard in 1506.

Greek writers described Phidias's other works of genius, which have since disintegrated or been destroyed. Among them were a huge gold and ivory figure of Zeus at Olympia and a vast bronze statue of Athene that stood on the **Acropolis** facing Propylaea. We know disappointingly little about Phidias, or about his methods of work, but his 'style' influenced Athenian sculpture until at least the end of the century. Large-scale projects like the Parthenon were, however, hard to carry through in times of war – when public funds had to be used for military purposes.

Domestic sculpture

Archaeologists often find small sculptures in people's graves. They show that sculptors did not just make huge statues, paid for by the city-state's government, to stand in public places. Sculpted household figures or objects could be ingeniously artistic – like pairs of **terracotta** feet that are actually little bottles of perfume. Sculptors brought to their workshops a wide variety of materials – ranging from marble, limestone and sandstone to gold, silver, lead, bronze and iron. They even worked in ivory, bone and **amber** – and made statuettes to be displayed in people's homes out of painted wood and beeswax.

The athlete

Athletic festivals, or Games, were held as a way of worshipping the gods. Only a big or rich city could afford its own stadium and the other facilities needed for a major Games. The four biggest were held at: Olympia (Olympic Games) and Delphi (Pythian Games) every four years, then at Corinth (Isthmian Games) and Nemea (Nemean Games) every two years. An athlete who won at all four major games was given the title *periodonikes*, or multiple champion.

These national Games drew full-time competitors and spectators from far and wide; many other Games were small-scale festivals just for local people. The events included sprinting; running in full armour; the long jump; throwing the discus and javelin; horse-racing and chariot-racing. As well as this, there were a range of highly-popular combat sports ranging from boxing and wrestling to *pankration* – a fearsome form of fighting (see box). All athletes competed without clothing.

This statue of a discus thrower shows the grace and beauty, as well as sporting ability, that were expected from Greek athletes.

Classical superstars

Ancient-Olympic champions won great fame. They were like modern football and movie stars rolled into one. Theogenes of Thasos, who won at over 1200 festivals, including three Olympic crowns, was worshipped as a god after his death. (A legend says that when an old opponent defaced a statue to Theogenes in Thasos, it toppled over and crushed him to death!) The best athletes travelled around from Games to Games, competing for glory and winning wreaths of olive or laurel leaves. These were like the gold, silver and bronze medals that athletes compete for today. However, they were not pure **amateurs**. For when they went home to their own city-states, they often received gifts of money or food from their fans and admirers. Therefore, unlike most people, they were able to eat plenty of meat to put on extra weight and muscle. Trainers and coaches paid very close attention to their athletes' diets as they prepared for big Games.

Athletes were always expected to compete honourably. At the big Games, competitors and officials alike took an oath to stick to the rules and neither offer nor take bribes. Cheating was then punished by whipping-men who were kept on standby. No one was supposed to forget that the prime purpose of athletics was not to win at all costs, but to show devotion to the gods.

Ultimate combat

Pankration (meaning 'complete strength' or 'complete victory') was an ancient-Olympic combat sport. Strangleholds; attacking the eyes; kicking; breaking fingers; dislocating limbs – all were used in an attempt to put down an opponent. Top *pankratiasts* were big men. The first Olympic victor, Lygdamis of Syracuse, was said to be a giant whose feet were 45 centimetres long. Such champions had to be determined too. There was no time limit to the exhausting fights, except nightfall, so *kartereia* or endurance was a good quality to have.

The actor

Like the athlete, the Greek actor did his work as a way of worshipping the gods. Plays developed from religious choral dances, in honour of the **deity** Dionysus. First one actor – usually the poet who had written the words – began to speak in **dialogue** with the rest of the chorus. This was made up of twelve to fifteen men. In later years, a second then a third actor, would come forward, while the chorus danced, sang and made running comments on the action. There were never more than three solo actors, and they were always men, since women were not allowed to perform in the theatre. In Classical times (roughly 500–300 BC), professional groups of actors toured Greece, performing wherever they were required.

Competitive drama

In Classical Athens, one of the year's greatest events was the springtime City *Dionysia* festival. Its main feature was a drama competition, lasting for four days in an open-air theatre that still lies on the southern slope of the **Acropolis**. Since it was a religious festival, the city government took a lot of trouble in organizing it and paying for it. The chief **magistrate** for the year chose which poets' plays should be performed; then he made sure that wealthy **citizens** paid for the training and costumes of the chorus.

On this vase from the 4th century BC, actors perform a comedy. They are wearing the masks and padded clothing that were typical for theatre.

These are modern versions of the kind of masks worn by actors in ancient Greece. Big masks were used to show everyone in a large audience clearly whether a character was happy or sad.

When all the plays had been performed – usually four per day – a panel of citizen judges voted on which play was the best. Then prizes were awarded not only to the poet and the actors, but also to the citizen who had financed the show. The festivals were hugely popular. Around fourteen thousand spectators crammed inside the theatre. They came from all walks of life, paying two **obols** to get in or nothing if they were poor. Women were not supposed to be admitted, but it seems that sometimes they were. Actors were pelted with stones or food from the audience's packed lunches if they did not come up to scratch.

First and best

The Greeks devised the first plays in the world and since some are still performed today, they must rank among the best ever written. Actors put on their masks to appear in tragedies (well-known stories about gods and heroes) or comedies (tales of everyday life). Tragic actors wore richly coloured, flowing robes and special boots called *kothornoi*. Comic actors wore lots of padding and flat slippers to make them look ridiculous. Unfortunately, of all the dramas written by playwrights like Aeschylus, Sophocles, Euripides and Aristophanes, only a fraction survives – but they do give us a wealth of information on life and attitudes in ancient Greece.

The thinker

'A life without asking questions,' said Socrates, 'is no life at all.' What he meant was *big* questions – about life, the universe and everything. Most Greek people were too busy in their daily jobs to spend much time pondering. However, a number of men were paid to devote their lives just to 'philosophy'. That is – thinking, investigating, discussing and exchanging ideas, and maybe even setting up schools to teach others to think for themselves too. Some of these philosophers were the greatest thinkers the world has ever known. Their ideas continue to influence the way we look at things in the 21st century.

World-class wise men

Before Classical times (roughly 500–300 BC), two notable thinkers were Heraclitus of Ephesus and Pythagoras, who set up a school at Kroton. Heraclitus believed that everything in the world is always changing. 'You cannot step into the same river twice,' he liked to say. (Think about that!) Pythagoras was a brilliant mathematician – we still use his ideas today. He was also a **mystic** who taught his pupils that the souls of the dead moved on into other bodies.

Sometimes Classical philosophers got into trouble by challenging existing ideas, especially religious ones. Socrates, the son of a stonemason, was told by the **Oracle at Delphi** that he was the wisest man in Greece. This baffled him, since he thought he knew very little. He decided that he must be wise because he *knew* that he knew so little. He sought to learn more by asking thought-provoking questions, but the Athenians decided he was corrupting the minds of his young pupils and sentenced him to death by drinking **hemlock**.

For a while Aristotle, shown in this mosaic, was a tutor to the future Alexander the Great of Macedon.

Schools of thought

Some thinkers attracted 'schools' of followers. The followers of Pyrrhon of Elis were called the Sceptics. They believed that people could be certain of nothing, so they should just try to be good. The Cynics who followed Diogenes of Sinope – an eccentric who lived in a barrel to show his hatred of worldly comforts and possessions – thought people should free themselves from all desire. Epicurus of Samos taught his Epicureans to seek happiness through self-control, while Zenon of Cyprus's Stoics – named after the *Stoa poikile* or painted porch in Athens where they first met – believed in accepting their fate, whatever it was, but trying to lead good and honourable lives anyway. Cynic, sceptic, epicurean and stoic are all words that we use in English today.

Socrates' pupil Plato and Plato's own disciple Aristotle set up schools which were the ancient-Greek version of today's most famous universities. Plato was concerned with how to produce good men and a good state. Aristotle was more interested in investigating and organizing man's knowledge in a practical way. 'The act of observation is what is most pleasant and best,' he remarked. Many of his writings have survived until today, ranging over subjects from politics and physics to biology and astronomy.

Plato is depicted in this statue. He wrote on many aspects of philosophy – often in the form of conversations which featured his old tutor Socrates.

The architect

The picture below shows the magnificent outdoor theatre at Epidauros. It is still used every summer, for modern audiences to sit on the same seats and see the same plays as ancient Greek people did, well over two thousand years ago. It was designed by the architect Polyclitus and built into the hillside in about 350 BC. According to the much travelled writer Pausanias, it was the finest theatre in Greece.

The Greeks liked to be surrounded by beauty, so they took a lot of notice of their public buildings – and of the men who designed them. In Classical times, the governments of city-states like Athens were prepared to pay for the best architects to give them the temples, theatres and treasuries they wanted.

The Athenians, for example, employed an architect for a new temple of Athene Nike on the **Acropolis**. An **inscription** from the first half of the 5th century BC recorded the appointment: 'Resolved by the council and assembly … a temple and a stone altar will be built according to specifications drawn up by Callicrates … Three men will be chosen from the council to assist him, and will indicate how the building work is to be **contracted** out.' In some people's opinion, work like Callicrates' has not been improved upon ever since.

The site of this ancient stone theatre is Epidauros in the **Peloponnese**. Earlier Greek stage buildings and seating areas were made of wood.

The quest for proportion

No specialist books on architecture survive from ancient Greece. The Roman architect Vitruvius did, however, pay homage to the Greek masters. 'The planning of temples,' he wrote, 'depends upon symmetry ... it arises from proportion (which in Greek is called *analogia*) ... Without symmetry and proportion no temple can have a regular plan; that is, it must have an exact proportion worked out after the fashion of the members of a finely-shaped human body.'

Architects worked miracles with great blocks of marble or limestone, cut out of Greece's plentiful quarries. They directed workmen to join these together with metal clamps and pins set in lead, not with **mortar** – making the joins almost invisible. They also used ingenious optical illusions to ensure that high buildings still seemed in proportion when viewed from below.

Uncovered by time

Builders were concerned only about the visible parts of buildings. Foundations were out of sight, so they did not have to be beautiful. When the Athenians decided to make a temple larger than in the original plans, their builders extended the foundations using any old stone that came to hand. Today, thanks to damage and **erosion**, some of this unmatched stone can be seen.

At the Erechtheion temple in Athens (see page 6), six statues of women – known as *caryatids* – took the place of columns to hold up the tops of the pillars.

How do we know? – The Acropolis

We know from Classical writings that a big *polis* would have an acropolis, a fortress in a high place, where the **citizens** could take refuge in times of danger. In 490 BC, or just before, the **Acropolis** in Athens was destroyed by the invading **Persians**. When the Athenians reclaimed their city, the citizens' assembly decided to pay for a new Acropolis – and they included an even more splendid temple than before, the Parthenon, which was built between c.447 and 432 BC.

'Eagle among the clouds'

Restored and repaired, the Parthenon still stands and, as well as astounding us with its beauty, it tells us a lot about the past. We can see the limestone foundations, the marble blocks so precisely shaped by stonemasons and the statues sculpted under the supervision of the great Phidias (see page 32). We can even read the annual building **accounts** for the whole project, inscribed on a pillar in the Acropolis. Those for the year 434–433 BC show that a balance of 1470 *drachmas* was carried over from the previous year, with 25,000 *drachmas* coming in from the treasurers of the temple of Athene, and various wages paid to workers 'for quarrying on Mount Pentelicus and loading stone into carts.'

The Parthenon looks like this today. The height of each column is four-ninths the width of the building. The width of the columns is four-ninths of the distance between them.

These are Parthenon roof tiles, which were fitted on to the wooden roof frame.

Buildings are made to last. So we know more about the work of ancient-Greek builders and architects than that of fishmongers, athletes, actors or certain other types of workers. From the writings of Plutarch, we even know the names of the architects who worked on the Parthenon – Callicrates and Ictinus. Today the Acropolis survives to be marvelled at. It is amazing to think that when the Parthenon first took shape high above Athens, on the streets below walked Greeks of such genius as Socrates, Hippocrates and Thucydides – alongside great numbers of the vital workers you have read about in this book. Athens, 'the eye of Greece, mother of arts and **eloquence**,' was fulfilling the prophecy of the **Oracle at Delphi**: 'You will become an eagle among the clouds for all time.'

An enduring achievement

The builders of the Parthenon would have been amazed at what happened to their great work. It later became a Christian church and afterwards, when the Muslim Turks made Greece a part of their empire, it was a mosque. The Turks then used it to store gunpowder and in AD 1687 an army from Venice blew it up during a war. Later Lord Elgin, a British ambassador to Turkey, got permission to bring many of the marble carvings to London – where they are still displayed in the British Museum.

Timeline

All dates are BC

c.3000	Greece controlled till c.1450 by Minoan kings based on the island of Crete
c.1600–1100	Greek-speaking Mycenaeans rule separate kingdoms in mainland Greece
c.1100–800	Period of wars and migration
c.800–700	Homer's the *Iliad* and the *Odyssey* probably composed; Greece made up of small city-states, ruled by separate kings or noble families
c.750–550	Greeks set up colonies in lands around Mediterranean
c.500	Some city-states become democracies with Athens the most powerful
c.490–479	Main period of **Persian** invasions of Greece
431–404	**Peloponnesian** War between Greek city-states, ending with Sparta eclipsing Athens as the most powerful state in mainland Greece
378–371	Sparta eclipsed by a new power – Thebes
336	Greece ruled by Alexander the Great of Macedon after his invasion and conquest
146	Greece becomes part of the Roman Empire

Sources

Ancient Greece – Utopia and reality
Pirre Leveque
(Thames and Hudson, 1994)

Classical Greece
Ed. Roger Osborne
(Oxford University Press, 2000)

Eat, drink and be merry
Audrey Briers
(Ashmolean Museum, 1990)

Europe – a history
Norman Davies
(Oxford University Press, 1996)

Greece and the Hellenistic World
Ed. John Boardman, Jasper Griffin and Oswyn Murray
(Oxford University Press, 1988)

The Greeks
Paul Cartledge
(Oxford University Press, 1993)

Political and social life in the Great Age of Athens
Ed. John Ferguson and Kitty Chisholm
(Ward Lock, 1978)

These were the Greeks
H.D. Amos and A.G.P. Lang
(Hulton, 1979)

Glossary

accounts financial records

Acropolis high-up fortress in Athens, where the citizens could take refuge in times of danger

agora market-place

amateurs players who compete merely for the love of sport, not for money

amber yellow fossilized material

anarchy lack of any kind of government

archaic primitive, long-ago

aristocracy rule by the 'best' citizens in a state

bailiffs officials (often in a court of law)

barbarians word used by ancient Greeks to describe anyone who was not Greek

barracks buildings where soldiers are lodged

beestings first milk of a cow after giving birth to a calf

character personality

citizens people in a democracy who were allowed to vote

civilization way of life common to particular groups of people

civil servants people whose job it is to help run a country or a city

colonies settlements in one place made by people from another place

contracted allocated to specialist workers in return for pay

cutpurse pickpocket, thief

deities gods and goddesses

democracies types of government by which people can elect their own rulers

dialogue two-way conversation

divulge speak openly about

drachma silver Greek coin, worth six *obols*

eloquence speaking fluently

erosion wearing away over time

frieze horizontal band of sculpture high-up on a building

hemlock poisonous potion made from a plant

hysteria uncontrolled, highly-emotional state

idiosyncracies personal peculiarities

indictments official accusation or charge relating to a crime

inscription words written on a stone, a monument or a coin

intrepid brave, daring

livelihood means of living, income

lyre small, harp-like instrument

magistrate officer in charge of enforcing the law

medlars fruits like small brown apples

metics foreigners, with some citizen's rights, living in a Greek city

meticulous very careful

mortar mixture of lime or cement, sand and water for joining stones or bricks together

mystic spiritual thinker

obol small Greek silver coin – six to a *drachma*

Oracle at Delphi holy place where people consulted their gods for advice or prophecies

overseers supervisor, foremen

palaestra open area for practising combat sports

pediments triangular part crowning the front of a Greek building

Peloponnese region of southern Greece, including Sparta (see map on page 5)

Persian person from an ancient Middle Eastern Kingdom, now known as 'Iran'

polis Greek word for city-state

precepts teachings, words of wisdom

quorum number of people who must be present to make official the decisions of any assembly

rustic country-dweller

shrines holy places

smelted removed from ore by melting

status position in society

subdivision specialized part or department

taboo forbidden thing

talent very large unit of Greek currency (6 *obols* = 1 *drachma*; 100 *drachmas* = 1 *mina*; 60 *minas* = 1 *talent*)

terracotta unglazed, usually brownish-red fine pottery

uppers part of a shoe that is not the sole

Utopia any ideal world

Index